LOST TREASURES

Treasure lies hidden all over the world — anything from rusty chests full of fabulous jewels to secret gold mines. Even as you read this, people are risking life and limb and investing huge sums of money in attempts to unearth pirates' loot, concealed centuries ago. Is it still there, or has someone else beaten them to it? Did it really exist in the first place? There is a fascinating tale to tell about each treasure trove, full of thrills and disappointments. Here are stories about six of the world's most famous lost treasures and the people who have tried to uncover them.

GREAT MYSTERIES

LOST TREASURES

John Wright

Illustrated by Bernard Long

The Bookwright Press
New York · 1989

Great Mysteries

Ancient Mysteries
Ghosts
Lands of Legend
Lost Treasures

Monster Mysteries
Sea Mysteries
The Supernatural
UFOs

Cover illustration: Captain Kidd watches some of his treasure being buried.
Frontispiece: The treasures of Lima, prior to being loaded on board the *Mary Dear.*

First published in the
United States in 1989 by
The Bookwright Press
387 Park Avenue South
New York, NY 10016

First published in 1989 by
Wayland (Publishers) Limited
61 Western Road, Hove
East Sussex BN3 1JD, England

© Copyright 1989 Wayland (Publishers) Limited

Library of Congress Cataloging-in-Publication Data

Wright, John
    Lost treasures/by John Wright.
        p.   cm. — (Great mysteries)
    Bibliography: p.
    Includes index.
    Summary: Presents twelve stories of real or
legendary treasure for which men have searched,
usually unsuccessfully.
    ISBN 0-531-18248-7
    1. Treasure-trove—Juvenile literature .   (1. Buried
treasure.) I. Title   II. Series.
G525.W915 1989
909—dc19

88-39273
CIP
AC

Phototypeset by Direct Image Photosetting Limited Hove East Sussex
Printed in Italy by G. Canale & C.S.p.A., Turin

Contents

Introduction	6
The statue in the sand	9
The riddle of the Buzzard	10
Digging for the Oak Island treasure	14
The "Money Pit"	16
The last words of Captain Thompson	20
The treasures of Lima	22
A vault filled with gold and jewels	27
The mystery of Rennes-le-Château	28
Hiding the Nazis' treasure	32
The hidden loot of Nazi Germany	34
Ambush in the Superstition Mountains	39
The "Lost Dutchman Mine" in Arizona	40
Conclusion	44
Glossary	46
Further reading	47
Index	48

Introduction

Buried treasure — words that send a shiver of excitement down the spines of people of all ages in every country. Mention them and we imagine a cutlass-carrying pirate swashbuckling his way around the oceans of the world, or a millionaire seated by the side of a swimming pool wondering what to do with the rest of the gold coins and jewels he has uncovered.

All sorts of people, from rich lords to thieves and humble priests, have put their valuables in secret hiding places for safe keeping. Some die without telling anyone where they are. Their belongings lie forgotten until we hear about the worker knocking down a building and discovering, quite by chance, a sackful of precious ornaments, or the farmer plowing a field and unearthing a cache of lots of gold and silver coins.

Long John Silver, the main character in Robert Louis Stevenson's book Treasure Island, *which is still read by people of all ages.*

Two British men with gold coins worth hundreds of dollars, which they uncovered while working on a building site.

Other people pass on maps and coded messages that give clues to where their treasure trove lies. Over the years, this information is copied and passed on from person to person. Mistakes creep into it, and descriptions of the clues, and even of the treasure itself, begin to vary wildly from what was originally said or written down.

Despite the unreliability of their information and the fact that they might be on a wild-goose chase, people all over the world keep on hunting for legendary treasures — most of them hidden centuries ago; some of them more recently. They put their lives at great risk exploring deep, unsafe tunnels and complicated networks of underground passages. They invest huge sums of money in projects that, more often than not, have to be abandoned with little or nothing to show for years of hard work.

Why do they do it? Is it just greed: a desire for fabulous riches? Or is it the challenge: trying to unravel an age-old puzzle created by someone who did not want his or her treasure found — ever?

Surrounding every hidden hoard there is usually a fascinating story about it and the people who have gone in search of it. Let us now look at some of the world's famous hidden treasures and the tales told about them.

A warning!

In his book *Nostromo*, Joseph Conrad wrote: *There is something in a treasure that fastens upon a man's mind. He will pray and blaspheme [swear] and still persevere and will curse the day he heard of it; he will let his last hour come upon him unawares, still believing that he missed it only by a foot. He will see it every time he closes his eyes. He will never forget it until he is dead — and even then — . . . There is no getting away from a treasure that once fastens upon your mind.*

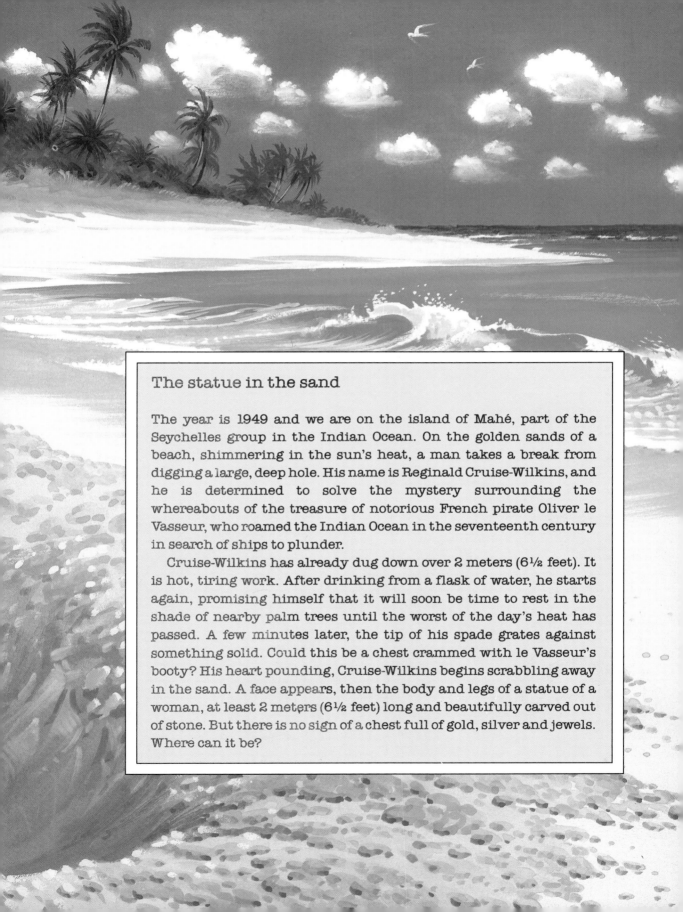

The statue in the sand

The year is 1949 and we are on the island of Mahé, part of the Seychelles group in the Indian Ocean. On the golden sands of a beach, shimmering in the sun's heat, a man takes a break from digging a large, deep hole. His name is Reginald Cruise-Wilkins, and he is determined to solve the mystery surrounding the whereabouts of the treasure of notorious French pirate Oliver le Vasseur, who roamed the Indian Ocean in the seventeenth century in search of ships to plunder.

Cruise-Wilkins has already dug down over 2 meters (6½ feet). It is hot, tiring work. After drinking from a flask of water, he starts again, promising himself that it will soon be time to rest in the shade of nearby palm trees until the worst of the day's heat has passed. A few minutes later, the tip of his spade grates against something solid. Could this be a chest crammed with le Vasseur's booty? His heart pounding, Cruise-Wilkins begins scrabbling away in the sand. A face appears, then the body and legs of a statue of a woman, at least 2 meters (6½ feet) long and beautifully carved out of stone. But there is no sign of a chest full of gold, silver and jewels. Where can it be?

The riddle of the Buzzard

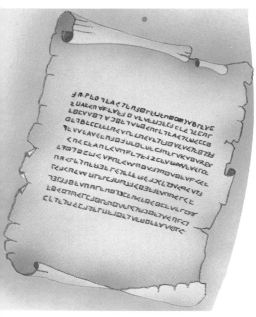

The Buzzard throwing his roll of parchment (see **above**) to the crowds.

Oliver le Vasseur, nicknamed *La Buze* (the Buzzard), was born in Calais in 1690. When the Buzzard was in his late teens, King Louis XV of France gave him permission to become a privateer. This meant that he could attack the ships of France's enemies so long as he agreed to share the captured treasure with his king. The Buzzard soon broke his side of the bargain and, hoisting the Jolly Roger, became a pirate in the Indian Ocean. He seized vessels from all countries, including those belonging to France.

Naturally, this enraged Louis XV and, in 1720, he offered a large reward for the Buzzard's capture. In 1730, the Buzzard was caught and sentenced to death by hanging. As he mounted the scaffold, he threw a roll of parchment to the crowds below and, with a loud laugh, shouted: "Find my treasure, to him who can understand!" On the parchment were twelve lines of writing, in a code, as well as some numbers and diagrams. Here were the clues to the hoard of treasure hidden by the Buzzard on an island somewhere in the Indian Ocean.

The Buzzard obtained most of his treasure from attacking ships in the Indian Ocean.

In 1756, the Seychelles Islands were taken over by a group of French people, among them the Savy family. They began to farm land in the Bel Ombre area of the island of Mahé. In 1920, one of their descendants, a Mrs. Charles Savy, noticed a curiously shaped rock poking out of the sea at low tide. Examining it closer, she found carved pictures of animals and a large eye on it. Intrigued by them, she asked some of her farm workers to dig beneath the rock to see if there was anything there. They discovered two coffins, each containing human bones and a pair of gold earrings, similar to those often worn by pirates. There was also an old pirate's cutlass next to the coffins.

Many pirates used to come to the Seychelles in the eighteenth century in search of fresh fruit, drinking water and timber to repair their ships. But was the Buzzard one of them? Mrs. Savy had already heard stories about him and now decided to find out if they were true. In her research, she came across an old map, printed in Portugal in 1729. On it, on the northwest side of Mahé, very close to her land, were the words "owner of land . . . the Buzzard." After making further inquiries, she also tracked down a copy of his roll of parchment. But try as she might, she could not decode the twelve lines of writing and the diagrams and numbers on it.

The cost

Cruise-Wilkins spent thousands in his search for the Buzzard's treasure. At one stage, he employed 48 people to help him, and the tiny island of Mahé echoed to the sounds of high-speed drills and the boom of explosives.

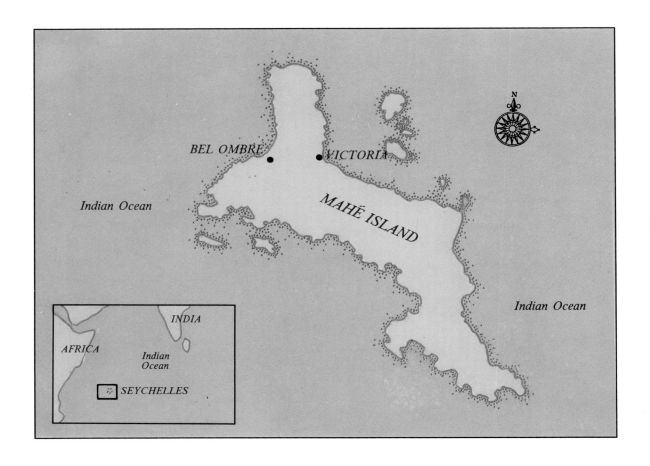

So the location of the Buzzard's treasure remained a mystery until 1949, when Reginald Herbert Cruise-Wilkins arrived on Mahé. An English farmer and game hunter from Nairobi, in Kenya, he came to the island to recover from an illness. He soon met Mrs. Savy and learned about the roll of parchment and the strange carvings on the rock on the beach. Fascinated by what he was told, he returned to Kenya with a copy of what the Buzzard had written in his pocket. He spent the next five months trying to unravel the mysterious words and diagrams.

Bit by bit, he translated the first of the twelve lines of writing, revealing the words: "a woman, waterlogged, dig at her feet." He was also able to work out a few other words and, as a result, deduced that the Buzzard was referring to the Twelve Labors of Hercules in Greek mythology and the constellations in the sky. He thought that the diagrams referred to bearings on a compass and distances. Full of excitement, he rushed back to the Seychelles to begin a search for the Buzzard's treasure that was to occupy him for the rest of his life.

The Buzzard's treasure was hidden in the Bel Ombre area of Mahé Island, in the Seychelles.

On Mahé, Cruise-Wilkins found his first clue: a flat, smooth stone with markings that looked like compass points. He was convinced that there was a connection between the stone and the Buzzard's diagrams. He paced out the distances given on the parchment, using the compass on the stone to give him the correct bearings. For several months he dug holes in different places, but without any luck. Then he uncovered the stone statue on the beach. As he stared at it in amazement, sea water seeped slowly through the sand and around the figure. He had solved the first clue! He had found "a woman, waterlogged."

Cruise-Wilkins worked on the Buzzard's parchment for the next twenty-eight years and solved all but the final line of writing. Each line contained directions to a buried object and a stone with a carving, which were used to solve the next stage in the Buzzard's puzzle. Eventually, after digging at many sites around the island, Cruise-Wilkins ended up at a point very close to where he had found the buried statue of a woman. He was sure that the last line would provide him with the answer to where the treasure lay buried.

Ill and penniless, after having spent all his savings in the search, Cruise-Wilkins struggled on, desperately trying to solve the final puzzle. He had discovered an underground cave with a carving on one of its walls of a sarcophagus (a coffin made out of stone) with a mummy lying in it. He was convinced that the treasure lay near it . . . if only he could untangle the remaining few words.

In 1977, he died before he was able to do it. With him went the information needed to solve the final clue to the mystery of the legendary treasure of Oliver le Vasseur, the Buzzard of the Indian Ocean.

A beach on Mahé Island, close to where Cruise-Wilkins spent most of his life looking for the Buzzard's treasure.

Digging for the Oak Island treasure

It is a sunny summer's day in 1795. Sixteen-year-old Daniel McGinnis has paddled his canoe across Mahone Bay in Nova Scotia, on Canada's Atlantic coast, to the island known locally as Oak Island. After beaching the canoe in a sandy inlet, he goes exploring. Soon he finds himself in a clearing, in the center of which stands an old oak tree. A weather-beaten block and tackle dangles from one of its branches, which has been cut short. Beneath it, Daniel notices that the ground has sunk into a saucer-like depression. Someone had once dug a hole there. Could this be the place where pirates had buried the treasure that is often mentioned by local people?

Back home, Daniel tells his two friends, Anthony Vaughan, aged 13, and John Smith, 20, about his discovery. The next day, equipped with rope, picks and shovels, all three return to Oak Island. When they have dug a wide hole, just over a meter (3 feet) deep, Daniel's shovel strikes a solid object – a layer of flagstones. Excitedly, the boys raise them, only to see loose earth underneath. But they are not disappointed, because finding the flagstones convinces them that something really does lie in the ground below them, so they continue digging. At a depth of 3 meters (10 feet), they come across a layer of oak logs, and another layer farther down. Realizing that it is too dangerous to go on, the boys decide to get help.

The "Money Pit"

After discovering the flagstones and the layers of logs, Daniel and his friends returned to their homes, in the town of Chester, and told their parents what they had been doing all day. The parents did not share their sons' enthusiasm for the hidden treasure and did all they possibly could to discourage them from returning to the island, even warning them that it was haunted. Not until 1804, nine years later, did the boys find a group of people who would provide the money for the equipment they needed to dig deeper.

By then, the walls of the hole had collapsed, but Daniel and his team soon cleared it out and resumed the digging. Three meters (10 feet) below the second layer of oak logs, another layer was found, and so it continued, with logs being unearthed to a depth of 27 meters (88 feet). The gaps between some of the logs were sealed with coconut fiber and ship's putty. At this point, a large stone was revealed, with

Ghosts

Oak Island is supposed to be haunted by the ghosts of pirates who used to visit it. In the past, strange lights and fires have been seen there, and a party of local people vanished when they rowed out to investigate them.

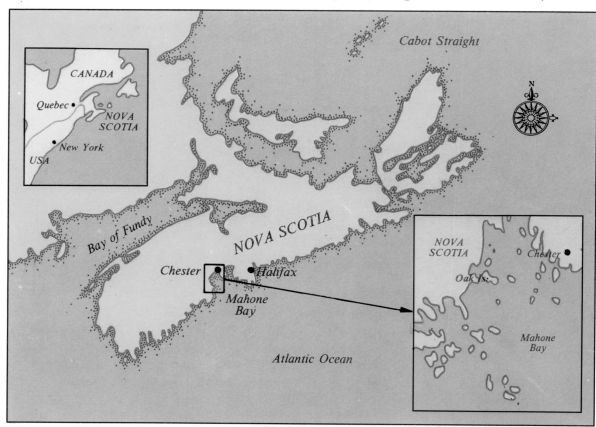

the words "ten feet below, two million pounds" in code on it. The diggers were convinced that they had almost reached their goal. They stopped, reluctantly, for the night. The next morning everyone was horrified to find their shaft flooded with water, almost to the top. Full of gloom, they began to pump it out. But despite all their efforts, the water remained at the same level. They tried again the following day, but it was no use and the project had to be abandoned.

Another attempt was made in the spring of 1805. The shaft, now called the "Money Pit," had caved in yet again, so the team decided to sink another one alongside it and then tunnel through to the old one. Just after they had broken through into the original shaft, the new one began to fill up with water. Once more, they admitted defeat and gave up.

Forty years later, in 1849, another group of people, called the Truro Syndicate, tried to reach the treasure. Anthony Vaughan was the only member from the previous teams to be involved. The Money Pit was dug out again until flooding stopped all work. This time it was decided to drill five narrow holes, 32 meters (105 feet) deep, to find out what

Above Daniel and his team at work on Oak Island (see the map **opposite**) in 1804.

The cost

To find the treasure on Oak Island: over $3,000,000 has been spent; over 20 shafts have been dug, and 6 men have lost their lives.

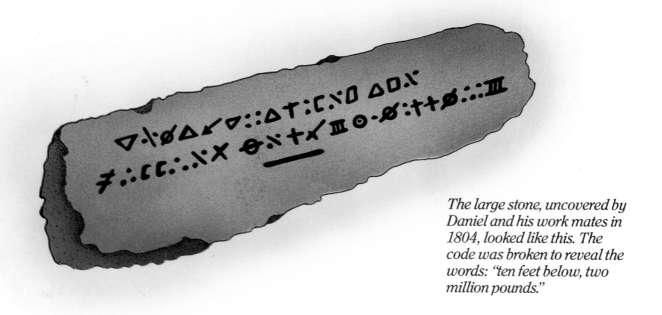

The large stone, uncovered by Daniel and his work mates in 1804, looked like this. The code was broken to reveal the words: "ten feet below, two million pounds."

was below the shaft. Samples brought up by the drills revealed that there were two oak chests down there, one above the other on a layer of logs. Encouraged by this news, which seemed to confirm that the Money Pit had been built to hide something valuable, a third shaft was dug to the west of the original one. It, too, became flooded. Where did all the water come from? By accident, a man fell into the shaft and swallowed what tasted like salty sea water. After a careful search around the shore of Oak Island, the syndicate discovered the entrance to an underground tunnel. It looked as though sea water, trapped in the tunnel, would flood the Money Pit if people broke the air-tight "seal" made by the layers of logs. Whoever had dug the Money Pit had been a very clever engineer. How could the syndicate keep the sea water from entering the tunnel?

Builders began constructing a dam to keep the water out of the tunnel. But the sea washed it away before it was finished. In desperation, dynamite was used to blow up the tunnel. Even so, water continued to flood the Money Pit. Disaster followed on disaster until the Truro Syndicate's money ran out. Once more, all work on the Money Pit had to cease.

Since 1849, many attempts have been made to find the treasure. In 1972, a team of treasure seekers sank a shaft to over 45 meters (150 feet). It, too, filled with water. Perhaps

The town of Chester, on Mahone Bay, where Daniel McGinnis and his friends lived.

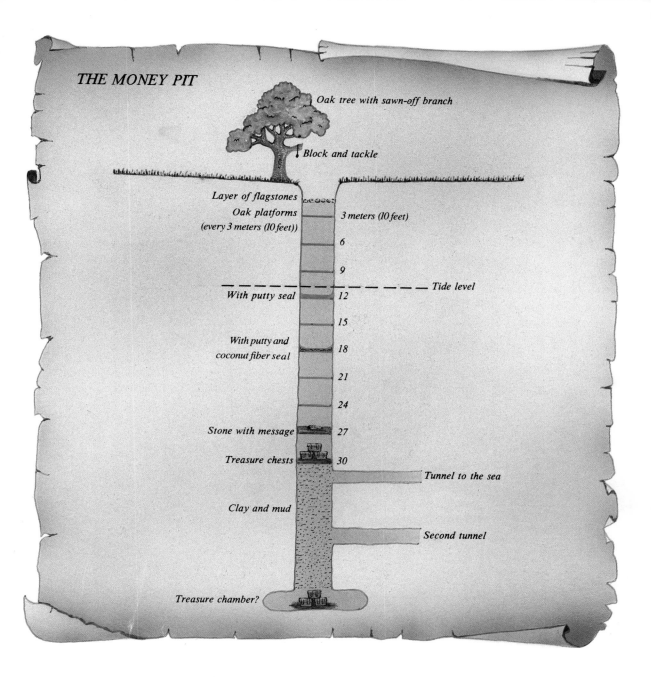

THE MONEY PIT

Oak tree with sawn-off branch

Block and tackle

Layer of flagstones

Oak platforms (every 3 meters (10 feet))

3 meters (10 feet)

6

9

Tide level

With putty seal 12

15

With putty and coconut fiber seal 18

21

24

Stone with message 27

Treasure chests 30

Tunnel to the sea

Clay and mud

Second tunnel

Treasure chamber?

A cross section of the main shaft of the Money Pit on Oak Island. Will we ever know what lies at its base?

there was a second tunnel beneath the first one? A special underwater camera was lowered. It showed two oak chests and a human hand . . . Is there a treasure chamber right at the base of the Money Pit?

Nearly 200 years after its discovery, all that has been recovered from the Money Pit are three small links from a gold chain. Many theories have been suggested about who buried the treasure, but Oak Island still holds onto its mystery. Local people say that when the last oak tree on the island dies, it will reveal its secret. Two still remain.

19

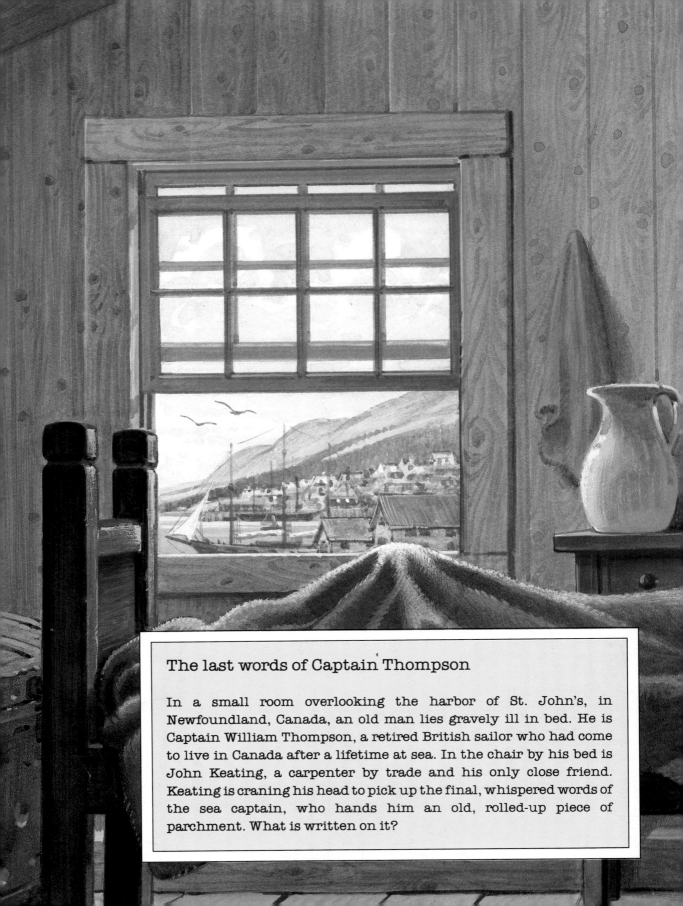

The last words of Captain Thompson

In a small room overlooking the harbor of St. John's, in Newfoundland, Canada, an old man lies gravely ill in bed. He is Captain William Thompson, a retired British sailor who had come to live in Canada after a lifetime at sea. In the chair by his bed is John Keating, a carpenter by trade and his only close friend. Keating is craning his head to pick up the final, whispered words of the sea captain, who hands him an old, rolled-up piece of parchment. What is written on it?

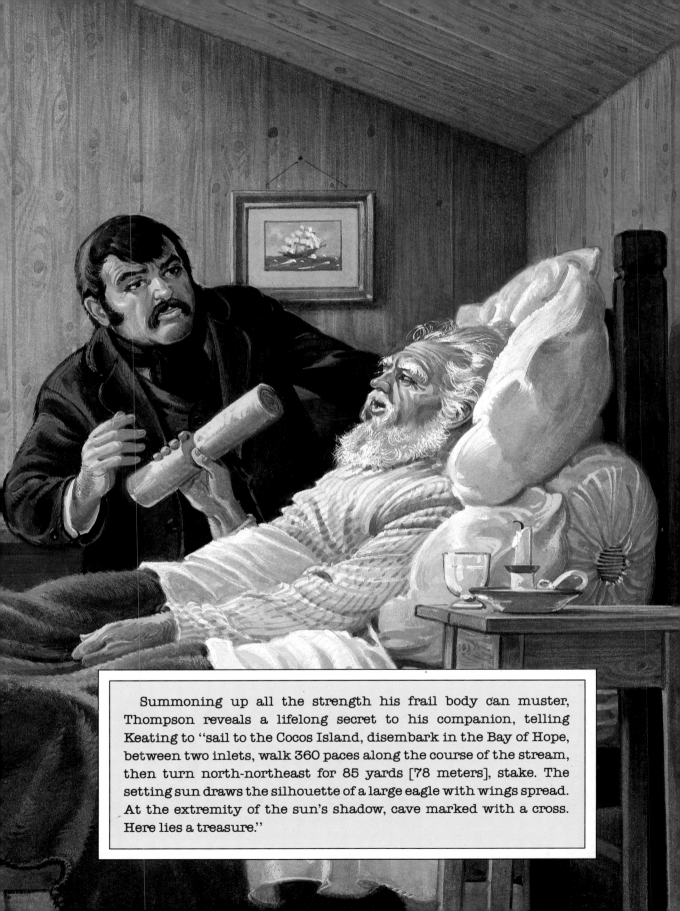

Summoning up all the strength his frail body can muster, Thompson reveals a lifelong secret to his companion, telling Keating to "sail to the Cocos Island, disembark in the Bay of Hope, between two inlets, walk 360 paces along the course of the stream, then turn north-northeast for 85 yards [78 meters], stake. The setting sun draws the silhouette of a large eagle with wings spread. At the extremity of the sun's shadow, cave marked with a cross. Here lies a treasure."

The treasures of Lima

In 1823, Lima, the capital of Peru, was under siege from Peruvians who wanted to overthrow their Spanish conqueror's government. At the time, Lima was one of the richest cities in the whole of South America because of the nearby silver and gold mines. Fearing that the huge amounts of gold and silver bullion held under his guard would fall into the hands of the rebel forces, the Governor of Lima decided to transport it back to Spain. So, along with the treasures of the city, it was taken to Callao, the nearest port to Lima.

Here, a British ship, the *Mary Dear*, was lying at anchor. With the rebel forces hard on his heels, the Governor pleaded with her captain, William Thompson, to allow him to store the treasure on board under the protection of the British flag. Thompson agreed; so Lima's enormous wealth was loaded onto the *Mary Dear* and guarded by some Spanish soldiers.

Captain Thompson was not a pirate, but he and his crew

A Peruvian worker in a silver mine near Lima, in the 1800s.

Lima's treasures being loaded onto the Mary Dear *in the harbor at Callao.*

had never seen so much gold, silver and jewelry, and the temptation proved too much for them. During the night, the guards were killed and thrown overboard, while the *Mary Dear* slipped anchor and set sail for Cocos Island in the Pacific Ocean, about 560 kilometers (350 miles) from Costa Rica. Far away from the main shipping routes, this uninhabited island was often visited by pirates in search of food and water. Some of them also hid their treasure there.

After anchoring in one of the island's bays, Thompson and his men took the treasure ashore, burying some of it and concealing the rest in a cave. The *Mary Dear* then headed back to the mainland. On the way, she was attacked by a

The *Mary Dear's* valuable cargo

The total value of Lima's treasure has been estimated at $36,000,000. It included a life-size, solid gold statue of the Virgin Mary, studded with 1,684 jewels; 11,000 precious stones, including diamonds, rubies and emeralds; 250 swords covered with jewels; 4,000 doubloons; priceless church ornaments; and the most valuable personal belongings of Lima's richest families.

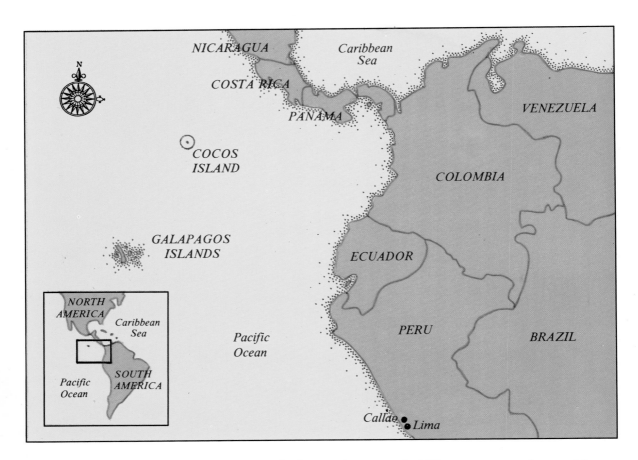

This map shows the location of Cocos Island, in the Pacific Ocean.

Spanish ship and captured. All her crew were hanged for theft and piracy, except for the captain and first mate, James Forbes, who were spared on condition that they reveal where they had hidden the treasure. They were taken back to the island. Here they escaped from their captors and fled into the thick jungle. Thompson and Forbes remained on Cocos Island for several weeks before being rescued by a passing fishing boat and returned to the mainland. Shortly afterward, Forbes died of yellow fever, leaving Captain

Other treasures on Cocos Island

Many pirates visited Cocos Island, two of whom are said to have buried treasure there. One was the British pirate Edward Davis, who unloaded seven boatloads of gold and silver sometime in the seventeenth century. The other was Bonito Benito, who is said to have brought $11,000,000 worth of booty to the island. In 1891, a man named August Gissler went there and stayed for seventeen years to search for Benito's gold. He discovered only 33 gold coins. In 1929, Peter Bergmans claimed to have found Benito's treasure, but when he returned to get it, he could not find the cave again!

Sir Malcolm Campbell visited Cocos Island to search for the treasure in 1926, but found nothing.

Thompson as the only person alive who knew where Lima's treasure was hidden.

Nothing is known about him until he reappeared years later in St. John's, Newfoundland. By then he was a sick man, and on his deathbed gave a map and instructions on how to find the treasure to his friend, John Keating. Keating passed all this information on to one of his friends, a Captain Boag. Together they sailed to Cocos Island. In 1841, they found the treasure, but quarreled over how it should be split up, and only Keating returned to their ship. The crew presumed that he had murdered his partner, although Keating claimed that Boag had drowned in a stream while trying to cross it laden with gold and silver. In all, Keating made three trips to the island and is reputed to have brought back $500,000 in gold. He died in 1894.

Since then several expeditions have gone to Cocos Island to locate the treasure. None has succeeded. Lima's wealth still lies concealed there.

The search for Cocos Island's secret

1823 Treasure taken there on the *Mary Dear*.

1841 Keating and Boag find it.

1894 Keating dies.

1926 The famous British racing driver, Sir Malcolm Campbell, visits the island for several days without luck.

1929 A French yachtsman, named Mangell, arrives with a map of the treasure's location, supposedly a copy of Thompson's original one. He goes away empty-handed.

1939 The great-grandson of James Forbes, first mate of the *Mary Dear*, spends a few weeks on the island, digging on one of its beaches. He leaves without finding anything.

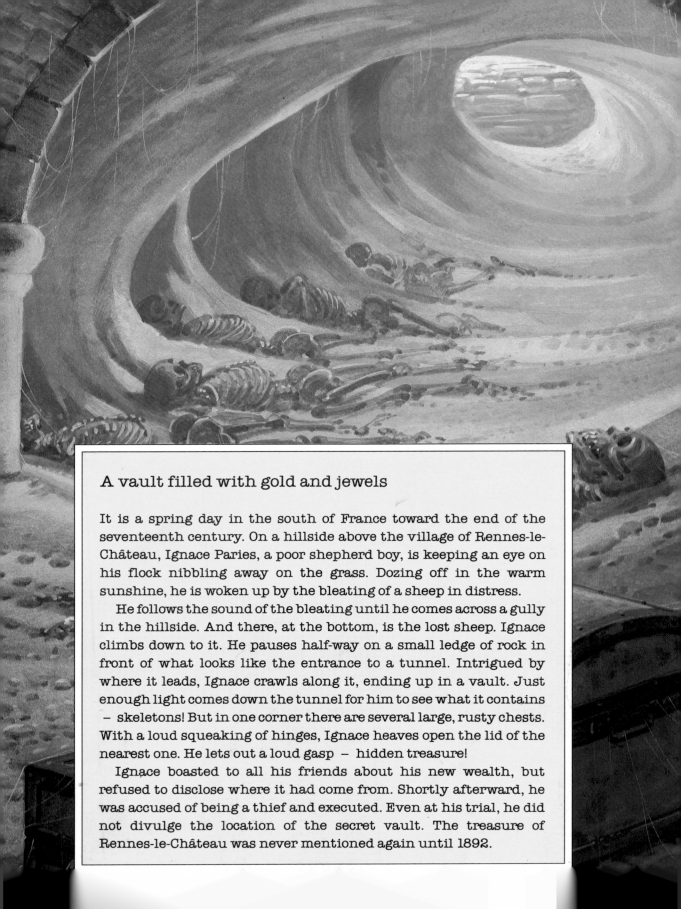

A vault filled with gold and jewels

It is a spring day in the south of France toward the end of the seventeenth century. On a hillside above the village of Rennes-le-Château, Ignace Paries, a poor shepherd boy, is keeping an eye on his flock nibbling away on the grass. Dozing off in the warm sunshine, he is woken up by the bleating of a sheep in distress.

He follows the sound of the bleating until he comes across a gully in the hillside. And there, at the bottom, is the lost sheep. Ignace climbs down to it. He pauses half-way on a small ledge of rock in front of what looks like the entrance to a tunnel. Intrigued by where it leads, Ignace crawls along it, ending up in a vault. Just enough light comes down the tunnel for him to see what it contains – skeletons! But in one corner there are several large, rusty chests. With a loud squeaking of hinges, Ignace heaves open the lid of the nearest one. He lets out a loud gasp – hidden treasure!

Ignace boasted to all his friends about his new wealth, but refused to disclose where it had come from. Shortly afterward, he was accused of being a thief and executed. Even at his trial, he did not divulge the location of the secret vault. The treasure of Rennes-le-Château was never mentioned again until 1892.

The mystery of Rennes-le-Château

***Above** A view of Rennes-le-Château in the 1800s. **Below** The local mason finding the hollow tubes in the altar of Béranger's church.*

Rennes-le-Château is a little village nestling in the Corbières Mountains of southwestern France. In 1885, Béranger Saunière became its priest and he employed a servant girl, Marie Denarnaud, to help him with his work. The two soon became inseparable and were seen together everywhere.

In 1892, Béranger obtained a government grant of 2,400 francs to restore his church's altar and roof. The local mason set to work to replace the damaged stone-work. When he was removing some of the old stone in the altar's columns, he came across four hollow, wooden tubes, each sealed with wax. He called the priest over and showed him what he had found. Béranger bent down and opened one of the tubes. Inside it was a roll of parchment with words written on it in a mixture of French and Latin. Béranger

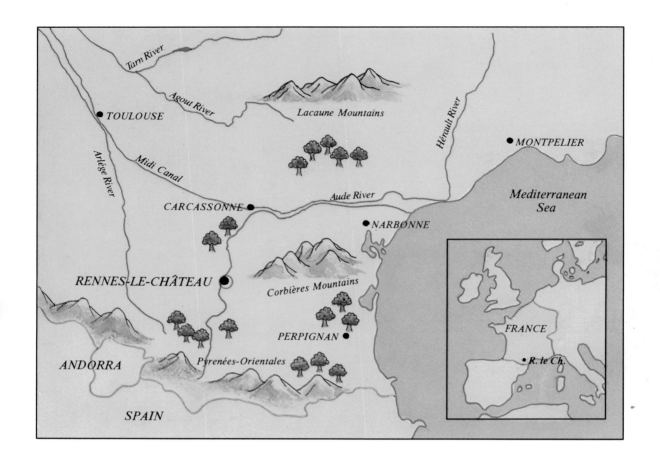

This map shows the position of Rennes-le-Château, in the southwestern corner of France.

assured the mason that it was unimportant and of no value, but he gathered up the rest of the tubes and took them to his rooms. Here he pored over the rolls of parchment for hours on end, trying to figure out what had been written on them.

On one of the parchments a sentence said: "The treasure belongs to Dagobert, King, and to Sion, and here he is dead." Another seemed to provide a mixed-up clue to where the treasure was hidden: "Shepherdess no temptation to which Poussin Teniers holds the key to peace 681 by the cross of this House of God, complete this Daemon Guardian at midday."

Putting the restoration of the church to one side for a while, Béranger went off to Paris, where he bought a copy of the painting *Shepherds in Arcadia* by Nicolas Poussin. It shows four shepherds around a tombstone. Béranger was convinced that it held a clue to the hiding place of the treasure mentioned in the parchments. When he returned to Rennes-le-Château, he confided his thoughts to Marie.

In the parchments, there were directions and distances from the church's altar to the treasure. Béranger and Marie

29

Shepherds in Arcadia by Nicolas Poussin. Did this painting provide the clue to the location of the treasure?

followed them, but found nothing. Meantime, Marie wondered if there was any connection between the tombstone in Poussin's painting and one in the church's graveyard for a certain Countess Hautpoul-Blancheford, which had strange hieroglyphics carved on it. She and Béranger set to work to decipher what they meant.

They must have been successful and located the treasure because restoration of the church resumed on a much grander scale than before. Expensive fabrics and gold crosses were bought for it — all out of Béranger's own pocket. Then, in 1897, he built a beautiful house, complete with rock garden and fountains, which cost him one million francs. He and Marie lived in it in great luxury. They wined and dined on fine foods and entertained all the important people of the area at expensive parties.

Word of this humble village priest's new lifestyle and behavior soon reached the ears of his bishop and the Mayor of Carcassonne, both of whom demanded an explanation. Amused by their concern, Béranger invited them to a sumptuous dinner party during which he told them that his new found wealth was a legacy from a long-lost relative in America. Then, before sending them home, Béranger gave them each an expensive gift. No more was said about his money.

On January 5, 1917, Béranger Saunière died of drink. Heartbroken, Marie shut herself away from the world for the next twenty years. When she became too frail to look after herself, a Monsieur and Madame Corbu moved into the house to keep her company. In 1946 Marie told them the story of the treasure hidden in a vault near the church, promising to tell them where the rest of it lay before she died. But, at the age of 86, she fell ill and quickly slipped into a coma, dying without regaining consciousness; so the Corbus never learned what became of the treasure of Rennes-le-Château.

Presumably it is still in the vault where Ignace Paries discovered it — or is it?

Béranger and Marie lived in great luxury in their new home, frequently giving splendid dinner parties for important people in their area.

Hiding the Nazis' treasure

In a forest clearing on a dark, moonless night in the spring of 1945, half a dozen German soldiers are unloading wooden crates from a truck, watched over by one of their officers, a Colonel Pfeiffer.

Some of the crates are very heavy. It takes four men to heave them off the back of the truck. As each one is placed on the ground, Colonel Pfeiffer goes over to it. He uses a crowbar to lever off the lid, then looks inside with his flashlight. Each time, his face is bathed in the yellow glow of light reflected from their contents – gold bars and coins; just a tiny part of the treasure looted by the German Army, during World War II from the countries they invaded.

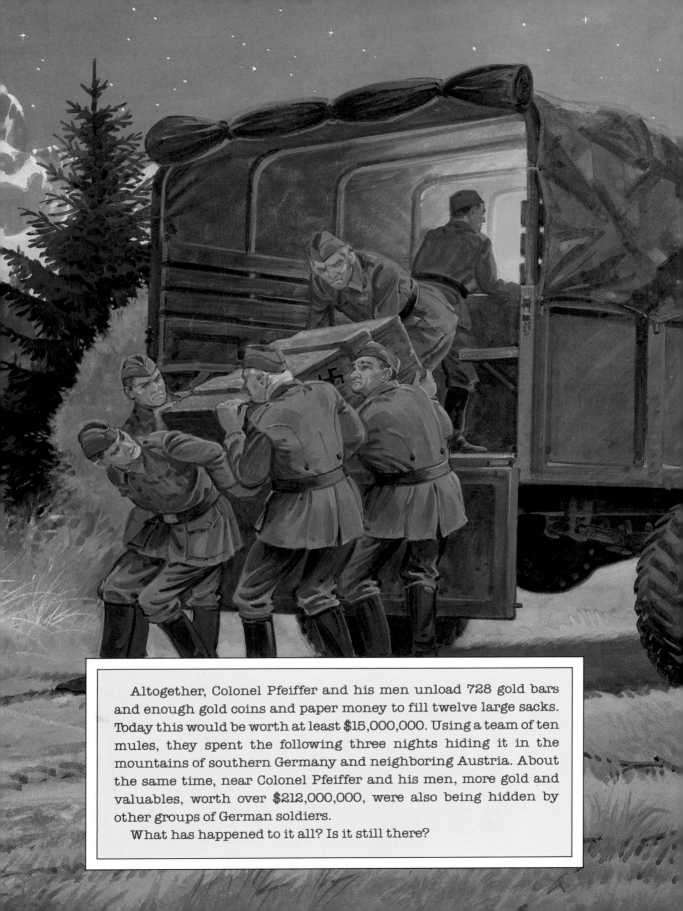

Altogether, Colonel Pfeiffer and his men unload 728 gold bars and enough gold coins and paper money to fill twelve large sacks. Today this would be worth at least $15,000,000. Using a team of ten mules, they spent the following three nights hiding it in the mountains of southern Germany and neighboring Austria. About the same time, near Colonel Pfeiffer and his men, more gold and valuables, worth over $212,000,000, were also being hidden by other groups of German soldiers.

What has happened to it all? Is it still there?

The hidden loot of Nazi Germany

Mountains along the border between West Germany and Austria.

During World War II (1939–45), the armies of Nazi Germany invaded France, Austria, Holland, Belgium, Poland, Hungary and Czechoslovakia, removing much of value from their art galleries, museums, banks and the homes of their rich families.

Most of this treasure was transported back to Germany and stored in the State Bank of Germany in Berlin. At one point, it has been estimated that this building contained gold to a value of $7,500,000,000 – a sum that excludes the paintings and jewelry also being kept there.

During a major air raid on Berlin in the spring of 1944, the State Bank was badly damaged by British and American bombers. As a result, Adolf Hitler, Germany's leader, gave orders for the bulk of the gold and other valuables to be moved to safer places in southern Germany and northern Austria. Other important Germans, who had their own hoards of treasure, were afraid that Germany would soon be defeated, so they, too, decided to transfer huge quantities of stolen treasures down to secret hiding places in the south, away from the Allied armies.

The mountains of northern Austria hold the clues to the final resting place of much of the Nazis' treasure. For instance, about 50 kilometers (31 miles) from Salzburg, near the town of Bad Aussee, treasure valued at $70,000,000 has been found in a salt mine. But what has happened to the rest of the treasure moved from Berlin? Many people have died in mysterious circumstances looking for it.

In 1946, two treasure hunters, Helmut Mahr and Ludwig Pichler, began searching in the mountains near Bad Aussee. They were found brutally murdered, a few weeks after setting

Where did it go?

In the chaos following the defeat of Germany in 1945, at least $50,000,000 of gold bullion and jewelry disappeared without trace from the State Bank of Germany in Berlin. Who took it: the Germans or the Allies?

Some of the Nazis' treasure has been found near Bad Aussee, in Austria. There is also thought to be treasure in Lake Toplitz.

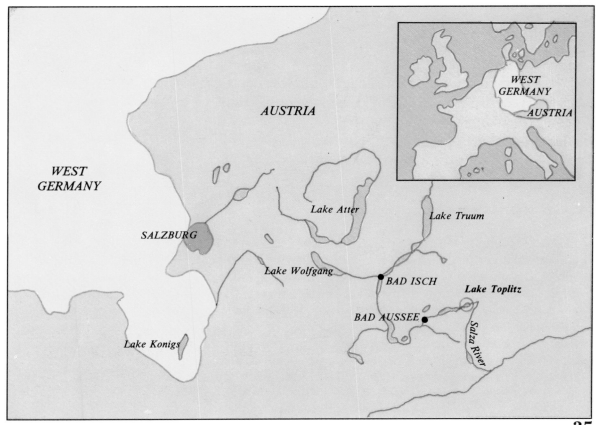

out. Near their bodies was a freshly dug hole and evidence that several chests or large boxes had been removed from it. What did they contain?

A few years later, Franz Gottlich, who had served in the German Army during the war, arrived in Bad Aussee and

Were two Austrians, Helmut Mahr and Ludwig Pichler, murdered in 1946 because they had discovered some of the Nazis' buried treasure?

Lake Toplitz's secret

Toward the end of World War II, members of the Austrian "resistance" movement followed a convoy of German trucks up a mountain road. They watched as 24 crates were unloaded, strapped onto the back of mules, and carried up to Lake Toplitz, where they were dumped into its cold, deep water. In 1959, divers went in search of them. All they could find were bundles of forged British £5 notes, which the Germans had used to pay their spies in England. In 1963, the Austrian government carried out a search of the lake. They only discovered some more of these fake notes. In 1970, two divers claimed to have found some silver plates in the lake, but they have never shown them to anyone. They also said they had seen several iron chests on the bottom of the lake.

An American soldier examines some of the priceless jewels found hidden in an Austrian castle. They were stolen by the Nazis from a rich family in Paris.

told everyone that he knew where some of the treasure was buried because he had helped to conceal it. Shortly afterward, he disappeared . . .

People began to say that the treasure was being guarded by descendants of the Nazis who wanted to use it to make the Nazis powerful again in Germany.

Much of the gold and art treasures stolen by the Nazis has been recovered and returned to the proper owners. However, the total amount still missing is in the neighborhood of $2,750,000,000.

A salt mine's treasure

At the end of the war, some American soldiers found the following treasure hidden in a German salt mine, deep underground:

- 7,000 sacks of gold coins, worth $126,000,000
- 8,527 gold bars, valued at $112,000,000
- 2,000,000 rare books
- 400 tons of priceless paintings and museum objects

Some of the forged British money found by divers in 1959 in Lake Toplitz. What else lies in this lake?

Ambush in the Superstition Mountains

It is 1864 and we are in the Superstition Mountains near Phoenix,
Arizona. Enrico Peralta is coming down a dusty track on a mule,
leading two more, each laden with gold ore. Three years earlier,
Enrico had been a poor farmer in Mexico. He moved to Phoenix,
Arizona, in the hope of a better life. Soon after his arrival, he began
to hear stories about people finding gold in the nearby Superstition
Mountains.

Enrico began going into the mountains for days on end,
convinced he would strike lucky. One day he returned and hugged
his wife, telling her that all their troubles were over. Whenever he
ran out of money, Enrico would return to his secret gold mine.
People warned him that this was dangerous because he was
trespassing on land sacred to the Apaches, but he ignored them. On
that fateful day in 1864, Enrico was thinking about the delicious
food waiting for him at home when an arrow thumped into the
ground nearby. Enrico never returned home.

The "Lost Dutchman Mine" in Arizona

Several years after Enrico's death, one of his relatives, Don Miguel Peralta, was rescued from a vicious fight in a bar in Mexico by two men — Jacob Waltz, nicknamed "The Dutchman," and a German by the name of Wiser. Grateful for his life, Don Miguel bought them many drinks and ended up telling them about Enrico's discovery in the mountains of Arizona. He also produced a sketch map drawn by Enrico, showing where the mine was located. Don Miguel suggested that the two men should help him find it.

So, in 1871, Don Miguel, Waltz and Wiser arrived in Phoenix, where they bought mules and provisions before setting off into the mountains. They returned with ore containing gold to the value of $70,000. Don Miguel went

The fight in a bar in Mexico during which Don Miguel Peralta almost lost his life.

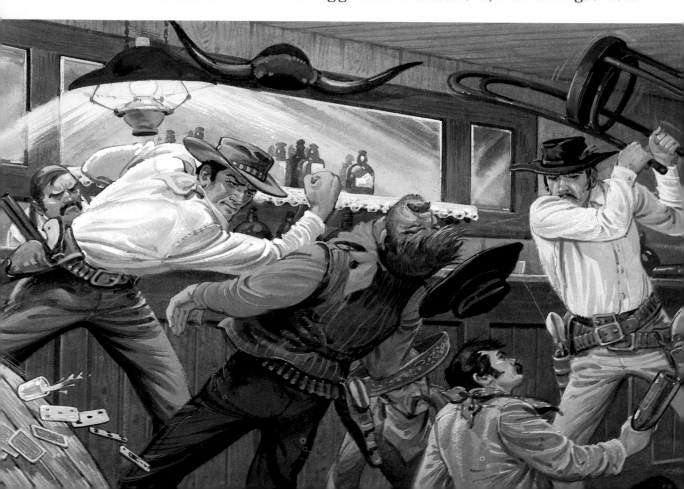

back to Mexico with his share, bought a farm and lived in comfort for the rest of his life. Waltz and Wiser gambled and drank their money away and decided to go back to the mine for some more gold. When they reached it, they were surprised to find two Mexicans — men who had worked for Don Miguel Peralta. A fight broke out, and Waltz and Wiser shot the two Mexicans.

Two weeks later, Waltz arrived in Phoenix — alone. He claimed that they had been attacked by Apaches. He had escaped death by hiding in a deep ravine, but his partner had "got shot full of arrows." Waltz was now the only person who knew the exact location of Enrico Peralta's mine. Soon after his return, he paid a considerable amount of money into a bank in Phoenix. A little later, he moved in with a Mexican women, named Julia, and lived a life of luxury, wanting for nothing. Whenever his money ran low, he would go back, alone, to the mine in the mountains.

In September 1891, Waltz, now 80 years old, became very ill and died the following month. On his deathbed, he told Julia how to find the mine in case she needed any money. Julia then summoned her father and brothers and

The Superstition Mountains are near Phoenix, Arizona.

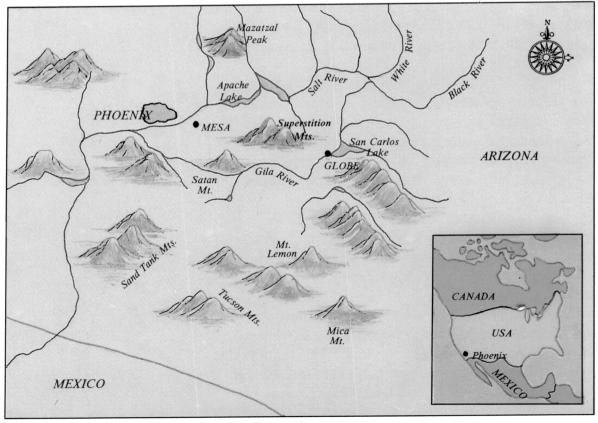

started to search for it. The instructions Waltz had given her were too complicated and they got lost. Time and time again they looked for it, but found nothing. Eventually they gave up and called it the "Lost Dutchman Mine" in memory of Jacob Waltz.

Nothing was heard of the mine until 1930, when Adolph Ruth set off to locate it. After he had been gone a month, his son sent out a search party. It could not find any trace of his father. Six months later, someone came across a human skull with a bullet between the eyes. A headless corpse was also found 2 kilometers (1 mile) away. The police decided that these were Adolph Ruth's remains.

In 1932, two treasure hunters in the Superstition Mountains were shot at by an unknown sniper, but escaped unhurt. Then, in 1946, James Cravey came to Phoenix and spent a lot of time gathering information about the mine. He became convinced that he knew its exact whereabouts, so, on June 16, 1947, he hired a helicopter to fly him to a canyon in the mountains. After unloading all his equipment and supplies, Cravey shook the pilot's hand, telling him: "I will walk out a rich man and will see you in Phoenix." He was never seen again. Several years later, James Cravey's headless body was discovered.

A valley in the Superstition Mountains.

In February 1951, Dr. John Burns of Oregon state was found shot dead in the Superstition Mountains while hunting for the treasure. Four years later, the body of Martin Zywotho of New York was discovered, shot through the head. In December 1959, the corpse of Stanley Fernandez, a gold prospector, was unearthed from a shallow grave; four days later, the headless body of Franz Harrer was spotted. In 1961, the skeleton of Himer Bohen was found. Another skeleton discovered in 1964 probably belonged to Jay Clap, who had been missing for three years. All in all, 44 men have lost their lives in this century while searching for the mine. Some of them died after getting lost and running out of food and drink, but most of them were murdered; the bodies of six were found without their heads.

Who killed them? Was it, as some people say, the Apaches, who do not want people on their land? Or is someone else jealously guarding the secret of the Lost Dutchman Mine? In spite of all these mysterious deaths, the search for the mine is continuing.

Gold prospectors, in the Superstition Mountains in the 1850s, looking for gravel containing gold.

Conclusion

Tales of buried treasure are told in countries all over the world. Some are true; others have been made up. Even with the true ones, facts have become confused over the years so that it is now difficult to know which are the correct ones and which are false. But this has not put off treasure hunters; spurred on by the thought of making their fortune, or like Reginald Cruise-Wilkins, by a determination to solve a centuries-old puzzle, they continue to search for that hidden chest of gleaming gold coins and sparkling jewels.

Every country has its secret hoard waiting to be discovered. In Peru, for example, the mystery of the disappearance of Pachacamac's treasure still has to be solved. Before the Spaniards conquered South America in the sixteenth century, the sacred city of Pachacamac, near Lima, contained many wonderful treasures. The huge doors of the Temple of the Sun, for instance, were made out of gold

Many of King John's crown jewels are thought to have been swept away by the rising tide, while he was crossing the Wash, on the east coast of Britain.

How many precious golden ornaments, like this Inca sun god, still lie hidden in the jungles of South America?

and studded with priceless emeralds; its altar, too, was built out of gold and surrounded with beautiful gold statues. When the Spanish general, Francisco Pizarro, and his *conquistadores* were at the borders of the Inca Empire, the priests of Pachacamac hid all their temples' precious decorations and ornaments because they had heard the invaders would steal them.

Most stories about buried treasure concern the pirates, filibusters and buccaneers who roamed the seas in the seventeenth and eighteenth centuries, attacking ships and robbing them of their cargoes. Perhaps the most famous pirate was Captain William Kidd, who plundered shipping in the Atlantic and Indian Oceans, amassing a vast fortune. What became of it? Most of it was probably hidden on islands in the Caribbean. One day, someone will come across it. At today's prices, it has been valued at millions of dollars. Another notorious pirate was the fearsome Edward Teach, nicknamed "Blackbeard," who terrorized the coast of North America. He is said to have stored his loot on an island in the Gulf of Mexico.

Not all hidden treasure is from the distant past. You have already read about the gold, silver and paintings concealed in Europe by the Nazis at the end of World War II; some more lies in North Africa, left by Field Marshal Rommel when he was fleeing from the British Army. It is said to contain gold, ivory and jewelry worth millions.

We can only presume that Rommel's treasure, like so many other hoards, has yet to be found, but we cannot be sure. Like everything else in treasure hunting, secrecy surrounds those treasures that have been discovered.

So no one is absolutely sure how much treasure is waiting to be unearthed. Nevertheless, the search goes on . . .

Undiscovered treasure

The Tower of London: some £7,000 is said to have been hidden in the cellar of the White Tower by a Colonel during the English Civil War.

Tuamatos Islands: Gold and jewels, weighing 14 tons, is said to be at the bottom of a lagoon on one of these islands in the Pacific Ocean. It was stolen from a church in Pisco, Peru, in 1849.

King John's crown jewels: King John is supposed to have lost these in the Wash, on the East Anglian coast of Britain, when his army was cut off by the incoming tide.

Glossary

Allies   The countries that supported Britain and America during World War II.

Block and tackle   A rope and pulley system for lifting heavy objects.

Booty   Stolen valuables.

Buccaneer   The name given to pirates in the Caribbean in the 1600s.

Bullion   Bars of gold and silver.

Cache   A hiding place for treasure.

Code   Signs or letters used for sending messages secretly.

Conquistadores   Spanish soldiers who followed Pizarro.

Cutlass   A short sword with a wide, curved blade.

Doubloon   A Spanish gold coin.

Eluded   Escaped.

Fabulous   Great; almost unimaginable.

Filibuster   A pirate who attacked Spanish territories in the West Indies in the 1600s.

Flagstone   A large flat, square piece of stone.

Forged   Faked.

Hoard   A secret store of treasure.

Incas   The Peruvian Indians who ruled the country before the arrival of the Spanish.

Jolly Roger   The pirates' black flag, which usually had a white skull and cross-bones painted on it.

Loot   Stolen valuables.

Mason   A person who builds things out of stone.

Nazi   A member of Adolf Hitler's Nationalist Socialist Party in Germany.

Parchment   A paper-like substance made from animal skins.

Pirate   A sailor who attacks and robs other ships.

Plunder   To rob.

Privateer   A captain given permission by his king or government to capture an enemy's ships and remove the cargo.

Putty   A soft paste that sets hard.

Ravine   A very deep, narrow gorge.

Resistance movement   Secret forces that attack an enemy occupying their country.

Captain Kidd, the famous pirate, watches his crewmen carry a treasure chest onto a Caribbean island.

Riddle   A puzzle.

Swashbuckling   Behaving in an aggressive and boastful way.

Treasure trove   Hidden gold, etc., that has been found.

Trespass   To go onto someone's land without their permission.

Vault   An underground room.

Weather-beaten   Damaged by the weather.

Wild-goose chase   Doing something that is a waste of time.

The White Tower, part of the Tower of London, where £7,000 is thought to be buried in its cellars.

Further reading

Donnelly, Judy. *True-Life Treasure Hunts*, Random House, 1984.

Furneaux, Rupert. *Buried Treasure*, Silver Burdett.

Green, Harriet H. & Martin, Sue G. *Treasure Hunts*, Good Apple, 1983.

Hamm, Monica S. *Dreams & Discoveries: A Coloring Book of Treasures*, Va Mus Arts, 1985.

McWilliams, Karen. *Pirates*, Franklin Watts, 1989.

Index

Apaches 39, 41, 43
Arizona 39, 40
Austria 33, 35

Bad Aussee 35, 36
Bel Ombre 11
Berlin 34, 35
Boag, Capt. 25
Buzzard, the
    see le Vasseur, Oliver

Callao 22
Canada 14, 20, 25
Cocos Island 21, 22-25
Cruise-Wilkins, Reginald, 9, 11,
    12-13, 44

Denarnaud, Marie 28, 29-30, 31

Forbes, James 24
France 10, 11, 27, 28

Indian Ocean 9, 10

Keating, John 20-21, 25
Kidd, Capt. 45, 46

le Vasseur, Oliver 9, 10-13
Lima 21, 44
Lost Dutchman Mine, the 40-43

Mahé Island 9, 11, 12, 13
Mahone Bay 14
Mary Dear 22, 23
McGinnis, Daniel 14-15, 16
Money Pit, the 16-19

Nazis 32-3, 34-7, 45
Newfoundland 20, 25
Nova Scotia 14

Oak Island 14-15, 16-19

Pachacamac 44-5
Pacific Ocean 23
Paries, Ignace 27, 31
Peralta, Don Miguel 40-41
Peralta, Enrico 39, 40, 41
Peru 22, 44
Pfeiffer, Col. 32, 33
Phoenix 39, 40, 41, 42
pirates 9, 10, 11, 14, 16, 23, 45
Poussin, Nicolas 29, 30

Rennes-le-Château 27, 28-31

Saunière, Béranger 28-31
Savy family 11, 12
Seychelles Islands 9, 11
Shepherds in Arcadia 29, 30
Smith, John 15, 16
Spain 22, 24, 44-5
Superstition Mountains 39, 42-3

Thompson, Capt. 20-21, 22-5
Treasure
    clues to finding it 10, 11, 12,
        13, 17, 18, 21, 29
    cost of looking for it 11, 17
    value of it 13, 23, 25, 33, 34,
        35, 37, 45
Truro Syndicate 17-18

Vaughan, Anthony 15, 16, 17

Waltz, Jacob 40, 41
Waltz, Julia 41-2
West Germany 32, 34, 35, 37
World War II 32, 34, 45

Picture acknowledgments

The publishers would like to thank the following for allowing their pictures to be reproduced in this book: Bruce Coleman Ltd 13 (Bruce Coleman); Mary Evans Picture Library 22, 26, 46; GSF Picture Library 34; Giraudon/Bridgeman 30; Peter Newark's Western Americana 43; Photri 18, 42; TOPHAM 7, 25, 37 (both), 47; South American Pictures 45 (Tony Morrison). All the artwork is by Bernard Long, except for the following by Marilyn Clay: 10 (upper), 12, 16, 18, 19, 24, 29, 35, 41.